Recognizing Your IMMENSE Possibilities

A UNIQUE APPROACH

Charles Albert Huth, B.S., M.Ed.

BALBOA.
PRESS
A DIVISION OF HAY HOUSE

Balboa Press books may be ordered through booksellers or by contacting:

Balboa Press
A Division of Hay House
1663 Liberty Drive
Bloomington, IN 47403
www.balboapress.com
1 (877) 407-4847

Print information available on the last page.

ISBN: 978-1-9822-3495-9 (sc)
ISBN: 978-1-9822-3496-6 (e)

Balboa Press rev. date: 11/05/2019

CONTENTS

DEDICATION

This book is dedicated to the Creative
Evolutionary Energy of the Universe.

PREFACE

This book is a unique approach to creating an extraordinary life. It weaves together universal principles, ancient wisdom, psychology and quantum physics in an easily understandable manner. Understanding the tapestry of life - which includes past, present and future, as well as the the physical and nonphysical elements of the universe - provides a pathway to live in harmony with all there is. Although, some of our prominent scientists proclaim that life is a mystery, we can learn to live in harmony with the mystery. If you make it a practice to trust and follow your internal guidance, it is very possible that you will end up in a situation beyond your fondest dreams. The reader can develop a strategy to achieve becoming his/her best self. It is a self-actualizing journey emanating from one's True Self.

PART ONE

CHAPTER 1

Creating an Extraordinary Life
with Your Natural Talents

Happiness and fulfillment are things that you can create for yourself. Would you like to dispel some of your fears and live as the captain of your ship? Throughout antiquity, there have been many expressions that basically stated, "change your thinking and your life will change." At first glance, this thought may seem absurd. However, when you consider that much of personal counseling deals with altering one's perspective to enhance positive change, the validity of this idea comes into focus.

We may think of ourselves as small fish in a big pond, with little importance or significance. As small fish, we seek comfort and protection from anything that could be harmful. We also tend to deal with ourselves as if we were the center of the universe, with everything revolving around ourselves. Contemplative thinking regarding where we came from, where we are going, and what is one's purpose in life, can appear puzzling and unsettling without further inquiry and scrutiny. These questions can appear to be obstacles to knowing one's True Self - but is this a valid concept?

Some days I consider myself smart, but there are other days that I question that assumption. I am a very busy person with many things I love to do. Often, I complain to myself that I have too many things to do, but at the same time I realize I would not be happy living any other way. Conflicts within myself, which may be many, are not always conscious. These conflicts limit my ability to express my passions compatibly, while reaching for my full potential. This ambivalence confuses my clarity of thought and creative actions. I become frustrated with myself. How can I recognize and utilize the many capabilities I have? What awareness do I need to expand the possibility of being all I can be? How would I know what I should or could be? Enlightenment on these confusing and complex questions can be enhanced by getting down to the basics of our existence.

Humans have much more in common than different. Although our differences are small, percentage-wise, each person is unique in terms of physical structure, culture, experiences, etc. These differences create unique perspectives that impact our lives. Therefore, there is no one philosophy, path, journey, or understanding that universally works for everyone. This may be one reason we use metaphors and fables -- to enhance our ability to see, understand and widen our perspective. In some regard, many of us live in a self-contained prison or box. Our thought processes are restricted by our false concepts of self and others. As I see it, I am working on expanding my personal prison/box. Throughout my life, many kinds of experiences have given me the opportunity to expand my understanding of self, others and questions regarding the nature of life. In other words, it was a variety of experiences and moments (including books, classes, counseling, conversations and the occasional epiphany) that broadened my perspective.

The universe conspires to help everything reach its
full potential. A blade of grass will work its way up
through the cracks of cement to be all it can be.

Four core principles or concepts to reveal your True Self

The principles or concepts described here can be viewed as tools to further open the door of self-awareness. There is a procedural hierarchy that can help facilitate this goal. At the top of this list is the concept of Oneness, which recognizes that everything is interacting with everything else as one entity. This leads to the use of your Intuition, which enables you to discover and know your True Self. Then, recognizing and Following Your Passions leads you to personal fulfillment.

If you are a "do-it-yourselfer" and you enjoy modifying and fixing-up your home, you may have a toolbox. If that is the case, you have some tools to make those creative changes. And so it is with your life. You can also select tools that you feel comfortable using to create desired modifications within you. Here are some basic principles (with instructions) to develop personal changes in your life.

One: Oneness

Oneness is a concept of reality that enhances one's ability to understand human dynamics. It is not an "airy-fairy" idea. If this is one's first exposure to this concept, skepticism in many forms is normal. However, with time and focused attention, the reality of Oneness can be incorporated into your daily perspective of life. One of the many benefits of this understanding is that when you are dealing with a situation where things do not appear to logically connect, you will sense there are missing pieces to the puzzle.

Modern science states that the physical world expresses as inter-reacting energies. It is important to recognize this interconnection/reaction between all things in the universe, including the nonphysical - or unseen. Thoughts are things because thoughts are a form of energy that has characteristics like other forms of energy – such as frequency, vibration, attraction, etc. It is a fact that brain waves can be measured. Our ability to think regarding past, future and current issues enable us to respond to the daily circumstances of our lives, allowing us to thrive in a good way. These thoughts/energy forms interact with other energies. To communicate with one's self and others, we must artificially separate things to provide an understanding of the issue at hand - this is a tree, and this is a house, or this is a leg and this is my body, etc. - while simultaneously understanding that there is no real separation of anything in the universe.

Everything reacts with everything else simultaneously. Creating and understanding facts is very important, and fortunately, our brain's right hemisphere can provide the appropriate context to use these facts. It is an ongoing activity. Anything alive is growing;

therefore, everything alive is changing. Furthermore, total brain input enhances our ability to thrive. Noticing how everything is interconnected provides the foundation for living in harmony with ourselves and the planet. If one makes a conscious decision to notice how things are interconnected, sooner or later you will have developed an internalized, functional perspective of Oneness. This new perspective brings clarity and peace of mind. We will pursue this matter with processes in the next chapters.

Many of us who think in terms of Oneness believe that there is only one mind and one soul that everyone shares parts of, just as we share the air that we breathe.

Two: Intuition

Intuition is a most important tool to develop and keep accessible. Intuition is another form of energy that you are endowed with. This inherent gift is available to everyone. It has been largely misunderstood and underused. First, let's consider what intuition is and is not. Intuition makes use of one's conscious mind, subconscious mind, passions of the soul, and life experiences to help formulate a direction to follow.

The province of the right hemisphere of one's brain adds to and evaluates left hemisphere input. It does not provide facts, as such. However, it does provide direction. It is more comprehensive than left hemisphere calculations. A set of facts may require additional ideas to determine the best way to beneficially use them. Ascertaining facts is a good thing to do, provided one understands the limitations that facts offer. We do not live in a linear universe. It may not be possible to calculate all possible outcomes and unintended circumstances regarding the cause and effect of any set of facts. Creating facts is the province of the left hemisphere of our brain. We live in a dualistic world -- something tall cannot exist without something short. Therefore, the scientific method of proving the truth cannot exist without its opposite. What might be the opposite of the scientific method? I say it is intuition.

The benefits of using your intuition are: a) It can take the guesswork out of situations where we cannot possibly know all the ramifications intellectually; b) it enhances one's feeling of being connected to all there is, with the added sense of well-being and comfort. One doesn't need to understand electricity to turn the lights on.

Building trust in using one's intuition is not difficult to do. Start with simple things, such as finding a parking place, or the correct route to travel. Essentially, you can learn to carefully listen to the voice in your mind, evaluate it and develop trust in that information. With dedicated effort over a period of time, you will build trust in your internal guidance. When tragedy or great difficulties appear in your life, you will have the confidence to make the best decision for you and yours. In Chapter 3, there is a detailed process that you can engage in that will help you develop a functional use of your internal guidance with trust.

I am often asked why I always appear to be happy, with an upbeat attitude. My response is: I trust my intuition to guide me through difficult situations and assist in the fulfillment of my heartfelt passions. I know that I am an integral part of my environment, which provides a sense of fulfillment and protection; it is an important component of my comfort zone.

Intuition is a skill that you can further develop. In the upcoming chapters you will be provided with tips and processes that will enhance the development of your intuition.

Three: Know and Honor your True Self

Ideally, we were born into an environment of love and joy, without excessive stress. Unfortunately, many of us did not have that optimum experience. Regardless of the wide range of human experience, a desire to love and be loved deeply impacts our lives. It is important to recognize that negative experiences offer us an opportunity to grow and achieve beyond our dreams and expectations. We express gratitude to those who will help us. It can be equally important to be grateful to those who present stumbling blocks. It is through overcoming stumbling blocks that our lives can be enriched. Developing an understanding of one's True Self requires effort and dedication. If we have a false perception of who we are, it is not probable that our life can reach its full potential or develop a sense of abiding fulfillment. Getting to know your True Self requires a dedicated pursuit that can take much time to achieve, and may take several years. This writing is partially dedicated to help you achieve this goal.

Four: Follow your Passion

One's heartfelt, soul-driven passion can be a guide to your well-being and a rich source of satisfaction and fulfillment. The soul is the animating and vitalizing principle in man. It is credited with the ability of thought, action and emotion; it is considered a non-material entity. For some, it is viewed as the spiritual aspect of being human, which is connected to All There Is. It is not a body part. The soul has a passion that it seeks to fulfill, which will provide benefits to the individual as well as to the community. The passion of your soul is a driving issue that affects your life. Your passion consistently seeks attention, and will continue to seek recognition and fulfillment. It is something that you cannot easily ignore. The lack of attention to one's passion can affect one's health. The body-mind is one entity without separation. Therefore, harmonious compatibility between body, mind and soul enhances healthy relationships and good health.

Your Journey into the Mystery

Our minds cannot contemplate all the unintended consequences of our thoughts and decisions. *It is impossible*! We do not live in a linear world. Everything is interacting with everything instantaneously. When we rely solely on our left-brain for guidance, it is possible to create undesirable outcomes. This creates stress with a byproduct that negatively affects one's health.

Our internal guidance provides a daily path and not a destination. The unknown destination can be viewed as a mystery. Living in the mystery can be very exciting because you do not know exactly where you're going. Focusing on your internalized, intimate relationship with All There Is allows you to feel guided and protected. Do not be surprised when you end up in situations beyond your wildest, fondest dreams. The universe conspires for everything to reach its full potential.

The following chapters are designed to help you internalize concepts that will enhance your ability to reach your full potential and live in an environment of peace and contentment. Creating a daily practice will assist you in this adventure.

CHAPTER 2

Consciously Internalizing the Reality of Oneness

Unless we are experiencing pain or malfunction in some part of our body, we think about ourselves and relate to the world as one entity. Even though we recognize that the ankle is connected to the leg, and the leg is connected to the hip, etc., we do not naturally think about ourselves as individual body parts. However, our body parts are constantly working in harmony as one entity, providing mobility to thrive and pursue our goals.

The human body cannot be separated from its mind, even though the mind is not a body part. How we think is an important element in addressing health issues. How we think is a very important consideration to creating good health and vitality. But this is not the end of the story. Our reality and quality of life is interdependent with our environment, which cannot be dismissed because it is a fact.

Quantum Physics as Related to Human Life

Modern physics describes life on our planet as different forms of energy interacting with each other. We know that some forms of energy have an attracting quality, while other forms of energy selectively repel each other. We know that the elements that comprise the human body are commonly found on earth. Quantum physics principles relating to human life include the following:

1. Everything is a form of energy.
    a. Energy cannot be created or destroyed, only transformed.
    b. Rocks, thoughts and electricity are examples of different forms of energy.
    c. Our body functions physically with electrochemical energy.
2. Everything is connected by energy. Therefore, everything functions as one entity.
    a. What happens to one member of a group effects everyone in the group. We are all interconnected.
    b. What happens to one part of your body affects the rest of your body.
3. There is an implicit order of growth in everything. This order of growth takes place in all situations; it starts with basic functions through maturity, and extends out into the world. Maturity is characterized as functioning at the highest level for the highest good for all, as one unit.

For example:

    a. Individual – conception, birth, stages of mental and physical development into maturity.

    b. Relationships - attraction, connection, commitment, and healing childhood wounds into oneness.

    c. Family - connection, basic needs, raising children, and maturity into oneness.

    d. Organizations - basic needs of the organization, development of goals and procedures, evolving into maturity where the highest and best good of each person and the organization become one.

4. Every set of circumstances is driven by its potential. Consider that every problem is driven by a solution. Problems contain a positive intent that is trying to emerge. The solution is calling you to your fully potentialized self.

    a. Relationship issues are driven by a need to grow into wholeness.

    b. Wars are conflicts driven by the need to fulfill full planetary potential.

Some examples of common energy interactions:

- Humans breathe in oxygen and breathe out carbon dioxide. Trees use carbon dioxide to create energy and oxygen. Trees provide humans with needed oxygen and use the carbon dioxide which is toxic to humans as a source of energy. This is a symbiotic relationship necessary for human survival. This demonstrates a symbiotic relationship between energies.

- Migrating birds do not use maps or weather forecast to know when and in what direction to fly. They have a built-in guidance system that connects to their environment. This could be considered a wireless connection.
- The human mind is not a body part. And yet, we use it to help guide and protect us. We create each day with our thoughts.

Daily, make it your practice to maintain the Oneness concept in everything you think and do.

CHAPTER 3

The Art and Science of Intuition/Internal Guidance

We cannot see the wind; however, we can feel it and accept this as reality. Intuition is similar. We can't see it, but we can feel it and see its effects. Just because something cannot be seen does not make it any less real. We can feel shifts in our energy. When we feel sad, we physically feel different as opposed to when we are happy. Our bodies feel less restricted when we are happy. We live in a world where everything is an expression of energy; it is to our advantage to learn how to use energy that is naturally available to us.

In the first chapter, it was stated what intuition is and is not. Clearly intuition does not generally offer facts to consider. Rather, it is a path to follow in order to safely navigate a complex world where all the consequences are beyond our ability to immediately comprehend.

It takes mindfulness and work, over time, to build trust in your ability to use internal guidance/intuition as part of your decision-making process. It is necessary to become comfortable with relying on your intuition for guidance. Remember, migrating birds do not need maps or a weather forecast. They have their own built-in intuitive navigational system to provide a safe journey. The bottom line is that thoughts are a directed energy that connects to other energies, each seeking its own potential. (Refer to quantum physics in Chapter 2.) We may not be able to control events; however, we can control how we think. How we think is a great asset to positive outcomes and our well-being.

As you engage your internal guidance, be aware that your journey will take you through difficult situations that appear undesirable and unwanted. Stumbling blocks offer opportunities for personal growth to enhance your journey into your full potential. Therefore, tragedies and other difficult times are not necessarily conflicted with your journey into your full potential.

The following is a process that you can use to develop your intuition and trust in its validity for you.

The Art of Listening

We are aware that language, whether spoken or written, can be misleading and confusing. The art and science of communication requires dedicated effort. *Listening skills are no less important than speaking skills.* Effective communication can be difficult. Therefore, when we are engaging our internal guidance, we must learn to effectively communicate with our source within. This is a skill that can be developed with experience, practice and time. Without building a proper foundation for using your intuition/internal guidance, you will not have a solid foundation to depend on during a time of extreme stress or tragedy, plus it may not be the appropriate time to solely rely on your internal guidance. Now, pick a quiet place and focus on the chatter going on in your mind.

- Do you hear one voice or a whole committee of confusion?
- Is the voice (or voices) loud or quiet?
- Is your body responding to the voice(s) you hear? Do you feel relaxed or do you feel a buildup of muscle tension?
- Asked the voice(s) simple questions regarding the concern/situation at hand until you hear a small, calm and peaceful voice. Your body will relax, and you will feel comfortable that the answer you hear is correct for you. This may take some minutes when you first begin to use this process.
- Beware of the possibility of asking a question that is not directly related to the issue or is too complex a question regarding the issue. Simple, direct questions are more successful.
- For me, I will only follow the advice of this calm and peaceful voice. If I cannot decide which voice is calmest, I will choose (if at all possible) to do nothing at that time. If you should find yourself in an emergency and are feeling panicky, you will be limited to the logical side of your brain. As you

develop confidence in listening, you will be less likely to panic in difficult situations.

- For some, their sense of feeling is stronger than their hearing sense. Always be alert to your body's responses to the answers you receive. A relaxed, calm body generally indicates the best choice for you overall.

As humans, we are known to have five senses that guide our behavior. They are the senses of sight, hearing, smell, touch and taste. These innate senses can, and often do, relate to past experiences. We process information intellectually with the left hemisphere of our brain. We can choose to engage our right hemisphere by using this Art of Listening technique or other similar processes. Our internal guidance allows us to correctly deal with a situation that goes beyond our intellectual capacities. Daily build trust with your internal guidance by using it with everything you think and do. Actively engage and maintain your internal guidance in all areas of your life.

CHAPTER 4

Who Are You? What is your Essence?

Although, humans are all basically the same, our culture, experiences and passions make life highly individualized for each of us. Some of us are classified as physically handicapped or mentally impaired; however, that does not limit one's capacity to be all that they can be. In other words, they are whole and complete within themselves. With that understanding, the only limitation may be how anyone thinks about themselves. If your concepts and thoughts about yourself place limitations on your life, how significant would that be to the quality of your existence? This could be an interesting question without an adequate answer.

Perceived limitations can be viewed as unnecessary obstacles. The beauty of diversity in humans is that, collectively, we can create a better environment for everyone to thrive, which would not be possible from one singular mindset or ability set. Due to limited self-awareness, the concept of True Self is often a daunting idea to embody. Embodiment refers to internalizing the thoughts and actions of your True Self. When we try to live up to the aspirations of others, we conflict with our true nature. This is a source of much unhappiness, often with the by-product of health issues.

Your only way to function compatibly with your True Self is to understand who you are, and become that Self by internalizing it - nothing else will work. The following are some ideas to facilitate recognizing your true nature. Be cautious of expecting quick results. Over your lifetime, many things have contributed to your misunderstanding of self and others; therefore, it takes time to develop awareness of these false perceptions. However, it is a journey with rich rewards.

Developing Self-Awareness

Understanding your True Self and the validity of your beliefs are necessary for your life to reach its full potential. Becoming aware of your false assumptions and any erroneous information can be a daunting task, but the rewards are many. Once upon a time the earth was considered flat. This belief created fear of falling off the edge of the earth, which is impossible. To us, this seems preposterous. Through our upbringing, culture, and experiences, we have created invalid assumptions and beliefs that guide our everyday lives. These misbeliefs will not allow you to be all you can be, because they are not based on the truth of your reality. Humans can be referred to as Meaning-Making Machines. We strive to give meaning to our lives and meaning to our experiences. The common perception is that we have some control over our lives through a better understanding of our experiences. The problem arises when the meaning we have given to certain sets of circumstances is not correct. Therefore, it is important that humans become aware of blind spots in their thinking and be aware of that as a possibility. If one has a specific mindset and hears statements from multiple sources that support that mindset, there is a strong tendency that these statements are considered factual when, in fact, they may not be. All of us need to scrutinize the validity of what we believe and what we hear. The truth can set us free to be all we can be!

The following are some thoughts that you can consider as you facilitate a better connection to your True Self:

1. Be willing to give up some things you think are true because, in fact, some ideas you have are not factual. Challenging what you believe to be true, along with introspection and reflection, are important aspects to connecting to your True Self.

2. There is no one perfect process to disengage your false perception of yourself and others. The information given here can stimulate an internal dialogue that can direct you to what you need to know.

3. Separation is about being at odds with your True Self and All There Is. When confronted with separation issues, it is a good time to evaluate your opinions about the circumstances that you are dealing with.

4. There is a truth that resonates from one's heart. It can reveal itself by entering the voice. Listening to the inner voice that speaks to you can be a developed skill. Our internal guidance reveals what we need to know. This resonance within our hearts has the power to disrupt our habitual patterns of thought and emotional responses which negatively impact our lives.

5. We can see in others what we do not necessarily see in ourselves. When you are bothered about another's behavior, notice if this is a personality trait you also share.

6. When in conflict, check in with yourself regarding your response and the validity of the motivation that is driving your action.

Unraveling the false perceptions of self is like peeling an onion, one layer at a time. It takes effort, time and is not always enjoyable. We know there is more than one way to get to Chicago; therefore, we have choices. And so it is with becoming aware of our true selves. I have found that journaling is an effective way to open doors into self-awareness.

A Case for Personal Journaling

Personal journaling is a primary source of awakening to intellectual creativity. When we verbally or mentally self-examine ourselves, it is easy to overlook the incongruities in our thought processes. However, when your thoughts are written down, it is much easier to review those thoughts and see the inconsistencies and the confusion they create. One benefit of journal writing deals with organizing one's thoughts to reveal the truth (or not) regarding long-held beliefs. Or to come to a coherent conclusion regarding the validity of issues at hand. Writing opens different levels of understanding, different from the verbal thoughts that created them. The process of journal writing is a most valuable tool for developing clarity and good ideas. It can be an important part of your journey into your True Self.

Our personality and perspectives were developed early in childhood. Childhood issues tend to remain in different disguises throughout our lifetime. Therefore, understanding ongoing personal dynamics allows you to make different choices in your response to life's circumstances. It is very difficult to create positive change if the underlying dynamics are not understood.

Journaling Areas to Consider

The goal is to create a comprehensive understanding of the dynamics of your family of origin and how that impacts your life today. Being successful in this endeavor can allow one to become free of limiting thoughts regarding oneself. Free to understand that everything is not preordained. Free to choose a life in peace and harmony, while fulfilling the passions of one's soul.

This is an arduous endeavor into unchartered waters. The level of your success will be directly proportional to the dedicated effort you put into it. There is not a linear path for you to follow. It relies on your desire to dig into your past and follow your guidance to what comes next, and then use this information to enhance your life.

Effective journal writing should be long enough to cover the subject but short enough to remain interesting.

The following is a <u>basic</u> list of journaling questions that can assist you toward your goal. Always be open to other questions that come to mind, which may assist you.

- What is hindering you from living an extraordinary life, the life of your dreams? Be as specific as you can. What do you believe an extraordinary life would look like for you? Describe in detail.

- What do you want to achieve in your lifetime (that you believe would give you fulfillment)? What do you feel your inner passions are? If you are not sure what inner passions speak to you, how would you figure it out?

- How do you think others view you? How do you respond to perceptions of others when they conflict with your self-perception?

- Describe the general nature of your parents, siblings, religious upbringing, and any family expectations that made a major impression on your life. When you think about the ongoing dynamics between you and your immediate family, what comes up most often?

- When you reminisce about your experiences growing up, what are you most happy about and how did that impact your life?

- List two of your most difficult childhood experiences in detail. Have you been able to move past these significant struggles or grief related to upbringing? If you have experienced a profound tragedy, how is that experience reflected currently? Were you able to find something positive in that experience to focus on?

- If you look back on your life experiences to date, do you see a common thread or pattern of reoccurring experience that could be an indication of your life's purpose? Describe this pattern/thread in as much detail as possible. Could this thread be the driving passion of your soul? Or could it be the emotional obstacle that is keeping you from living an extraordinary life?

- What have you done that created some of your proudest moments?

- What do you believe could enhance your ability to reach your full potential?

- How do you think you'll benefit by journaling these questions as well as other questions that come to you?

The Passionate Soul

The soul is defined as the animating and vital principle in man. It is credited with the ability of thought, action and emotion and is considered a non-material entity. For some, it is viewed as a spiritual aspect of being human that is connected to all there is. It is not a body part. I believe the soul has a passion that it seeks to fulfill, which will benefit the individual as well as mankind in general.

No one is an isolated island unto themselves. Each of us has a function and a passion to contribute to the greater planetary good - simply because we are an integral part of the whole planet. Our deeply held passions, when pursued, enhance the world in which we live. To connect with one's true passion requires contemplation of self and taking the time necessary to know our True Self. Socrates said a life unexamined is a life not worth living.

Connect Consciously to Your Soul's Passion

Often, I have asked the question, "What is your purpose in life, or what is the passion of your soul?" Surprisingly, many people do not have an answer that satisfies them. They will say, "I have thought about that, but I haven't come up with a satisfying answer."

So now, take a moment to reflect, consider and set an intention.

1. Find some quiet alone time to reflect on your life.
2. Set your intention to become aware of your deepest passions.
3. Think about and write down the various activities/skills that call to you.
4. Look for the common denominator in your life work and activities.
5. Do not expect instant success. The consideration of your thoughts requires adequate time and space.
6. The verification of your soul's passion will come with a calm, quiet voice and a relaxation in your body. Possibly an 'aha' moment! Continue your contemplation of self and taking the time necessary to know your True Self. Repeat as needed.

Your Soul is the Animating Part of Your True Self

The core principles and concepts of this endeavor are Oneness, Internal Guidance/Intuition and Knowing Your True Self, which together provide the foundation of this journey. Following the Passions of Your Soul will bring you peace and fulfillment. Do not be surprised if you end up in a situation beyond your fondest dreams. The remaining chapters are supplemental information to assist you on your journey.

A Daily Practice to Internalize:

1. Make it your daily practice to maintain the Oneness concept in everything you think and do.
2. Actively engage and maintain your internal guidance in all areas of your life.
3. Diligently determine who you are at your core.
4. Embody integrity at all times. Be a product of your word.

Although there is not a process that is perfect for everyone, one needs to start somewhere. Establishing a daily practice can be more than helpful; it will help you internalize your immediate goals. At the same time, more significant insights will emerge, enabling you to gradually transition from your false identity to your True Self.

PART TWO

INTRODUCTION TO PART TWO

In the first four chapters, we constructed a foundation to create your new extraordinary life. The following sections contain articles to assist you in your magical journey into the real you and your unlimited potential - the person you were meant to be! Life is a mystery. However, we can learn to live in harmony with it. You are the only one who can determine the validity and value of your life. It all starts with you.

Essential Concepts:

Living Life in a Mystery
Entanglement
A Fundamental Paradox
The Energy of Words
Fruitful Conversations
Integrity as a Structure
Embracing Personal Agreements

Charles Albert Huth, B.S., M.Ed.

Self Examination:

Personal Antagonist

Mirrors and Fears

The Masking of the Truth

Help! It's My Issue

Baby Steps to Forgiveness

The Blessing in Suffering

Understanding Healing Through Oneness

Creating Your Path:

Transitioning the In-Between Times

The Journey is the Destination

The Path to an Extraordinary Life

Daily Practices That Can Enhance an Extraordinary Life

ESSENTIAL CONCEPTS

Living Life in a Mystery

Questions regarding where we came from, where we are going, and what purpose each of our lives serve remains largely unsettled. Humans have a deeply seated desire to understand and give meaning to the nature of their existence. These kinds of questions have been pondered from antiquity to present time. If one requires absolute truths to resolve these kinds of questions, then the answers will remain elusive.

The physiology of the human body is well mapped out and generally understood. The human body is made of elements commonly found on earth. However, a surgeon will not explore a body searching for its mind. The mind is known to be a nonmaterial entity. We also know that the mind is used to help create the kind of life we choose to live. To answer the question – *What is and where is one's mind?* - requires a precise definition. However, by its very nature it also requires a degree of speculation. The dictionary definition of "mind" is: the element or complex of elements in an individual that feels, perceives, thinks, wills, and especially reasons. This definition does not depict the location of one's mind or its physical components, if any. As an analogy, we cannot see the wind but we can feel the wind and see the effects of the wind - and so it is with the functioning of our mind. We also know that we can harness the wind to create electrical energy. We also know that the mind can be used to benefit or harm humanity; therefore, it is incumbent on all of us to use this gift to enhance our lives to be compatible with all of humanity.

There is a theory that supports the idea that there is only one mind. It is described as a universal energy that exchanges information with everything in and on our planet, which is very much alive and active. In other words, the use of our mind is the conduit for a dynamic exchange of information that links us to our universe. Each person affects his/her environment and, in turn, is affected by the same environment; it is interactive. We know that the air we breathe is a shared commodity. The same relevance can be applied to our shared use of the mind. The mind is something we cannot physically see but, we can hear and see the effects of change generated by those who share similar goals or "like-mindedness." The use of our mind allows us to think about past and present events, and also allows us to contemplate future events.

The questions arise: *What drives us to do some things and not others? What motivates us to care for each other, to maintain ancient wisdom, and to understand the parameters of our being?* The soul is deemed to be the activating drive of our existence, over and beyond survival. The dictionary definition of soul is: the immaterial essence, animating principle, or actuating cause of an individual life. Or it can be the spiritual principle embodied in all rational and spiritual beings, or the universe. As used here, spiritual refers to the interconnection of all things. The soul makes its presence known as deeply held passions. Some would say it is also a heartfelt passion. Consider one's personal connection to the soul as their contribution to humanity. Therefore, each of us has an important role to support the general welfare. Supporting the human soul at large stimulates the evolutionary drive of consciousness on our planet. As a result, our technological drive grows exponentially. As a word of caution, we need to remain connected to our true human core and not let technology or materialism replace our humanity. If the passion of one's soul is ignored, this passion will continue to make its presence known. The result of this can include unintended consequences.

To protect and improve our humanitarian instincts requires personal diligence. Developing clear concepts regarding one's True Self (that personally resonate as Truth) will contribute to a world that can work for everyone.

Entanglement

Entanglement is a term used in physics that can be applied to understanding human behavior. It refers to a physical aspect of the universe. When something was unified and then separated, regardless of the length of time and separating distance, an energetic connection remains. This phenomenon is a good example of the concept of Oneness. We do not live in a linear universe, everything is interacting with everything simultaneously. Therefore, the idea of real and total separation of anything is an allusion.

Many years ago, experiments were conducted with blood samples. A vial of blood was taken from a volunteer and remove to another location. Using video cameras, clocks and other electronic equipment the volunteer and the blood sample were viewed simultaneously. The volunteer was placed under some stress and instantaneously the stress would show up in the blood sample. The bottom line is that the volunteer and his blood sample remained energetically connected regardless of distance between them.

The practical aspects of this phenomenon are endless. It supports the benefits of praying, that praying is a form of energy revealed in our interconnectedness. Before the Berlin Wall came down, groups all over the planet were praying simultaneously for peace. Knowing that group prayer creates a magnified energy, I got up at 4 o'clock in the morning to pray simultaneously with many people across this planet. Shortly after that, the Berlin Wall came down - something that was not expected.

The positive consequences of networking with like-minded people seeking a common objective also include each person's current or past personal relationships. Like the wind that cannot be seen, but can be felt and shown its effects, the contributing energy that each person brings adds to the impetus of the group's intentions. It is a way of extending support for one's current passions. This also includes the energetic support from our ancestors. There is a school of thought that states: *It only takes a small percentage of like-minded groups scattered around the world to stimulate positive change on our planet.*

Personal relationships are an important aspect of human development and well-being. Quality and trust are important to supportive and satisfying relationships. Relationships that are less than satisfying can be considered undesirable or harmful. When you consider that there can be some good found in everything you begin to realize that stumbling blocks offer opportunities for personal growth. All relationships have the possibility of value, the choice we have is how we respond to them. Self-examination regarding one's contribution to existing relationships is something we have control of and is vitally necessary. Accepting abuse from another is not appropriate and there are times when others are not interested in harmonizing their relationship. We all have our own blind spots. In these cases, one must accept that they tried their best without condemning them. I try to be aware of any blind spots, where I might not have awareness.

It is important to realize that a terminated relationship, regardless of reason, remains energetically connected no matter how hard we try to bury it. This is called *entanglement*. Time and distance will not break this bond. Having empathy or compassion for the issues of others is a good way to stimulate better outcomes. It is easy to have empathy for someone missing a limb. It is harder to feel empathy for someone who is emotionally damaged. We are more visual in accepting others, which limits our capacity to feel compassion. A lack of compassion can evolve into hate for another which creates a self-inflicted wound.

It is impossible to walk in someone else's shoes. My mother grew up in an extremely difficult environment. Her only defense was trying to make the adults feel guilty. This is how she tried to control her environment for the rest of her life. "My son you must not love me. Otherwise you would not have done that." She lived in fear, even though my dad took very good care of her and protected her. Making others feel guilty was part of her personality. This character trait of my mother was very troubling to me. As a result, I tended to feel guilty about my actions and feelings, which were not logically justified. I was in adulthood before I understood where these feelings came from. I always felt that she could overcome her childhood experiences and live in a better way but that did not happen. At the same time, I realized that if I had experienced life as she did, I may not have done as well as she did. Once I realized that my mother did the very best that she could do, I was able to let go of my judgmental view. Judging others harshly is detrimental to one's self. When we give up on judging others and focus on how we are engaging life, better outcomes can be assured. This kind of *entanglement* was a negative energy that affected my life until I understood the truth. Being judgmental can be a call to personal irritations of oneself that lie below our level of awareness. Every set of circumstances is driven by its potential.

A Fundamental Paradox

Many spiritual-minded people strive to live in accordance with principles associated with being God-like. God is considered omnipresent, omnipotent and omniscient. Philosophically approaching the paradox under consideration, I must assume one reason we are here is to learn lessons. Lessons can provide the opportunity to creatively enhance our lives. Our desire to live without internal conflicts and unresolved questions is an ongoing pursuit. A desire to learn more about everything and resolve our questions may be conflicted with our ability to divinely and deeply love ourselves. On the surface, we are sure that we love ourselves. However, at a deeper level we have a drive to improve and keep searching for more information - which is conflicted with being Godlike!

Being self-critical has at least two sides: It offers us a choice to be better and, at the same time, it may be a barrier to deeply loving ourselves. We continue to strive to learn more about our existence, what our purpose is, and increase our ability to become a better person. In other words, we notice our perceived shortcomings, which are conflicted with our idea of God-like qualities that we subscribe to. As a species, this may be a fundamental paradox that propels us towards our creative evolutionary drive in the universe.

It is said that a life unexamined is a life not worth living. Therefore, examining one's own life is relevant to how one conducts their life. In other words, one must come to the conclusions that resonate and satisfy their inner being. This individual enlightenment often coincides with a quiet small voice in one's mind and overall muscle relaxation.

You are part of the evolutionary development of the human species. Therefore, any effort on your behalf has positive consequences for our society. Striving for absolute perfection may be impossible and is certain to create stress. Pursuit of perfection in moderation can be a good thing and supports the evolution of our species. Some of us feel that we have a degree from the school of hard knocks, which has its benefits. These propensities for self-improvement and increased knowledge help energize a creative evolution into our personal and planetary potential. There is an added sense of fulfillment when you recognize that you are contributing to something larger than yourself.

The Energy of Words

It is said that thoughts are things. This concept theorizes that thoughts create a supportive energy to create manifestation. This intention can be expressed verbally or nonverbally. For example: I express that I want to go to a store - and then I find myself going there. In this case, my word becomes my reality. If you find yourself in a store, shopping without having the intention to do so, a cognitive disconnect could be a concern.

Let's look at the human being as an energy form. Physically, the human body is made up of various energy systems. These systems work as an integrated whole, communicating together to sustain our physical bodies. Mentally, our thoughts interact with each other and our environment. What we think about and what we perceive impacts our reality. If one is expecting a good day, that expectation will influence how one approaches their day, which impacts the outcome.

The human being is a remarkable creature in countless ways. Probably most of us do not think of ourselves in this way. Most of us do not spend much time thinking about how uniquely talented we are or how we impact our environment. When we look at those skilled in gymnastics, we get a glimpse of what the human body is capable of. Mentally, we have the capability of thinking about the past, present and future in detail. However, many of us may not think about the energy created by our intentions and how it changes our daily lives. Each word, statement or thought creates an energy that has consequences. The cause and effect of each word can range from the benign to the highly consequential. There is an energy that is created with each form of human expression.

Words are Palpable

Whether we are having happy thoughts or sad thoughts, notice the change in our bodily sensations, along with the shift in energy. Humans experience a wide range of emotions. Each emotion releases a different energy and, therefore, has its own unique manifestation. Each emotion simultaneously creates an energy shift in one's body and mind. Words and thoughts create emotions that stimulate palpable energy shifts in the body, along with observable body language. Nothing is really hidden; these shifts in energy are also palpable by others. Psychologists tell us that there is nothing hidden in any family. Although young children cannot intellectually verbalize what is going on, they have a sense of "hidden" conflicts. Any attempt to deceive another will, in the long run, not be successful. When someone's words do not reflect what they are truly thinking, a confusing energy is created that can bring unintended consequences. Nothing positive can develop from this disconnect, this separation from others.

Attachments to Words

If someone was expressing their love for you while hitting you on the head with a baseball bat, you would have a negative reaction to the word "love." Love would take on a different context for you – it would become a word you would not want to experience or hear. In this example, the word "love" was distorted and experienced negatively as fear. Although this is an extreme example, creating a strong emotion to specific words is not uncommon when it is differentiated from common usage. When a seemingly non-toxic word creates an over-the-top emotional response, there is something within oneself that is itching to surface. A need for healing and clear understanding is making its presence non-verbally known. It is equally important to be aware of one's own words or ideas that can have a significant emotional impact on others, exercising careful consideration without attaching a negative judgment.

Hidden Agenda Words

Having a conversation with a hidden agenda can be a recipe for disaster. At best, it is an act of dishonesty. When words are used deceptively, a meaningful conversation is not possible; therefore, a meeting of the minds is not possible. There is little chance to build consensus.

Cognitive Disconnection

A cognitive disconnect occurs when what we say and believe is conflicted with our actual thoughts and actions. This can occur in all kinds of situations. As an example: My dance teacher will tell me that I have counted the steps properly, but that is not how my feet moved, which comes as a surprise to me. There are those who honor a high level of integrity and honesty but get creative when it comes to filing their taxes. One way or another, cognitive disconnects are part of the human condition.

If one wants to function at peak performance, it is necessary to become aware of one's unconscious level of cognitive disconnects.

Communication Energy Transfer

Everything is energy. It is impossible to have a conversation without an exchange of energy. This energy exchange impacts both participants. If someone expresses how much they enjoy your company, but they really don't, the energy interchange will be negatively impacted. This will be true whether either party is consciously aware of it. Many of us can feel, can sense with discomfort, this lack of integrity. If one's goal is to have an effective conversation, resulting in the highest and best good for everyone, then openness and honesty is required.

Words can be differentiated by intention. Often the words "How are you?" are used to simply acknowledge the presence of another person. A much different energy is created if the intention is to inquire about another's well-being.

Everything is energy and everything is connected by energy. Each of us radiates energy that *can* influence and *be* influenced by the energy of others. Consciously use words to shift energy for the common good! The life you live is the lesson you teach.

A change in thinking can change your life!

Fruitful Conversations

A conversation has two parts, expression and listening. Both aspects of communication are equally necessary to achieve the best possible outcome. Yes, it is an equal partnership. It is very frustrating when a breakdown in communication occurs, creating a misunderstanding. Deep inside the human psyche is a need for self-expression, to be known and understood. For this to happen, the listener must be focused on the content of what is being spoken. The most effective basis for listening centers around understanding the communicator's point of view. In other words, there is a possibility of learning something new. When we listen to another while thinking about our own response (when he/she is through talking), we are not really listening. At some level, the speaker will know that you are not fully listening and, therefore, feel frustrated or annoyed. Our words, mannerisms and actions create an energy that goes with the spoken word.

Think about what it is like when you have a conversation with another, resulting in clarity of the issue at hand. That does not necessarily mean that you have achieved total agreement; however, understanding the perspective of another offers the possibility of ultimately improving the issue at hand. Our experiences and culture influence how we perceive the words we hear. Often, it is necessary to define words or ask for definitions from another. Some of our common words have more than one definition or cultural influence.

When you focus on one word in a sentence and assume that you have the correct context, you also assume what the speaker is trying to convey. The odds of you coming up with a correct understanding is minimal; therefore, a breakdown in communication occurs. This is referred to as *selective listening*. When one focuses on one word in a sentence that has a personal significance, a misunderstanding is highly probable, creating a false interpretation of the thoughts being expressed.

Our politicians commonly express half-truths. This is comparable to the idea that you are either pregnant or you're not, there is nothing in between. Therefore, we are better off when we deal with the truth and nothing but the truth. It is said that the truth will set us free. Human lives are complicated. Each of us looks at the situations around us from different perspectives. When we understand and accept the perspectives of others, a fruitful conversation is enhanced.

As a listener, you must do your part to help create effective communication. You must listen to learn, without projecting your biases and perspectives on the presenter. This will support clarity; a meeting of the minds is more probable. If nothing else, a better understanding of the speaker's perspective may illuminate a different solution. Yes, it is possible that your perspective can be changed if you allow yourself to truly listen. And to listen without a personal agenda!

Integrity as a Structure

Integrity as a human structure refers to the total integration of one's life. This integration of body, mind, actions, thoughts and soul-driven passions needs to be in harmony with what you believe. Hopefully, your principles are compatible with those ideals that support one's ability to thrive and support a healthful community.

In common usage, a lack of integrity often refers to a lack of good morals. Morality is a word that means different things to different people. Many associate the word "morality" with treating others honestly. That understanding of morality is only part of one's integrity. I am referring to integrity as a structure, a code - much like a building code. Building codes are used to ensure safety and purpose of function so that the structures are built to last. If some building codes are not adhered to, the integrity of the entire building can be at risk - and so it is with our human structure. On the surface, you may think of yourself as perfectly honest, but if that is not totally true, it is possible that you are not fully aware of it. That lack of coherence will try to make its presence known however it can, if only as an irritation. The universe conspires for everything to reach its full potential.

Your word is one aspect of your personal integrity. If you commit yourself to eating healthier and exercising more, but you do not follow through on that commitment, you have weakened the power of your own word. Similarly, if you make commitments to others and do not follow through on those commitments, you have weakened the power of your word. Your word becomes less meaningful to yourself and to others. This leaves one's integrity challenged.

> *What you say and what you do needs be in*
> *alignment with what you believe.*

Personal integrity is specific to you. Your integrity is based on aligning your life experiences with what you believe to be true. Personal integrity as a structure can be created by design. The question becomes: What do you want to create? Your creation should be a conscious decision. If not, your integrity may be based on your illusions. Your personal integrity should be based on principles that support all of life. Only you can find and connect with the principles that resonate with your True Self. These principles, when fully internalized, become your natural way of being. Then, if you "fall off the wagon" you will be instantly aware of doing so and can act to return to full integrity. Contentment with oneself is a very satisfying feeling. However, our sense of integrity can change as we mature. Remember, anything that is alive is growing and, therefore, changing.

Embracing Personal Agreements

Embracing personal agreements can increase self-awareness and stimulate better relationships. Relationships can be significantly improved with a few guidelines. It is through our relationships that the understanding of self is significantly enhanced. Honesty is a paramount consideration. When total honesty is not adhered to, complete understanding is not possible. If some aspects of the truth are hidden, an effective conversation is not possible. Without total honesty, you cannot be known for who you truly are, though you have an innate desire to be known. This is an unhealthy conflict that should not be maintained.

Making assumptions about another can also have unintended consequences. The possibility that an assumption is factual has a low probability of being correct. To make matters worse, it is common to treat assumptions as factual. If you maintained a record of each time you've made an assumption, you'd probably be shocked!

Taking things personally is equally problematic to your well-being. Often others are upset and project their issues unto you - unintentionally or intentionally. These issues really have nothing to do with you. If you document each time you take something personally, you will understand the pervasiveness of this problem. Evaluating the circumstances of our lives in this manner leads to relationship breakdowns.

There can be trust issues around speaking honestly. We fear that, if we are open about our thoughts and feelings, this information could be used to harm us. We fear that others will lose respect for us. We fear stepping into the unknown. Taking a risk has an uncertain outcome in the short-term, but in the long haul, being yourself will position you for a positive outcome. Therefore, some bravery is required to risk exposing who you truly are.

Your personal agreement to always speak honestly, not to make assumptions about others, and not to take comments directed to you personally will greatly improve your relationships. With a devoted daily practice of focusing on these agreements, it can become the natural way of living your life.

SELF EXAMINATION

Personal Antagonist

It is generally believed, by those who think about such things, that humans go about their daily routines without making significantly conscious choices. For a daily routine, they may decide when and where to go shopping, which would be considered in the automatic response category. Whereas, something outside of one's daily routine, such as an emergency, dealing with an unusual situation, or planning a vacation, etc. would require more of a conscious mode of thinking. Nonscientific estimates contend that humans spend much of their day with routine behaviors. This percentage is perceived to be in the high 90% range. Conscious (out of the box) decisions conceivably may average less than 5% on any given day. Like many things, there is value on both ends of a continuum that deals with automatic behavior responses and thoughtful conscious decisions. Therefore, both should be acknowledged and respected for the derived benefits of each. Playing the piano or dancing complicated routines without creating automatic muscle responses may be impossible. However, it is not uncommon for humans to unconsciously react to situations in a manner that restricts their ability to thrive and live in harmony with oneself or others. In other words, some of our routine behavior patterns can negatively impact our life.

Many of these ingrained, problematic behavior patterns are concealed by what is known as 'blind spots.' Blind spots refer to areas of one's life that lack awareness and are associated with negative behaviors that create unintentional consequences. If one is aware of the driving source of their negative behavior patterns, then they can choose to modify their behavior by selecting a modality that feels appropriate. Dealing with unconscious and troublesome behavior patterns is the focus of this writing. Consider this: It is difficult to resolve a problem without identifying its source.

Is it possible that one can have a personal antagonist, real or imaginary? The answer is yes! These kinds of relationships can unconsciously drive harmful and unwarranted behavior patterns. A personal antagonist need not be currently in one's life, or even alive for that matter. Nevertheless, this relationship remains active and thriving. This active relationship - with its accompanying stress – may be harmful to only you. The person who is the focal point of your upset may not even be aware of the stress you suffer.

Your personal antagonist is someone from your past (or present) whom you have elevated to a permanent role in your life. He or she could be a parent, a sibling, a former friend, or an employer. This was once a competitive relationship where your needs were not satisfied. Consequently, you have never stopped obsessing or competing with your antagonist. This is a situation where you cannot win.

A personal antagonist can be created by a variety of perceived conflicts that were never resolved. The issue of abandonment (which includes the loss of a loved one or absentee parent), seeking the love of an emotionally unavailable parent, or a relationship where feelings of not being good enough (or not smart, or attractive enough, etc.) were generated are common examples of how a personal antagonist can develop.

Your perceived antagonist could've been a well-intended person who meant you no harm. In some cases, there are those who lack a connection to their best self and engage in repetitive conflict. Whichever the source, this need for resolution is persistently, subconsciously driven within you. Until this issue is resolved, new relationships will appear, offering you a similar opportunity as the original stressor, to bring closure to your repetitive behavioral pattern. These new relationships will continue to form until one recognizes the source of the underlying dynamic. The universe conspires for everything to reach its full potential; therefore, these stumbling blocks will make their presence known until they are resolved.

Abraham Maslow was known as a humanistic psychologist. He believed that everyone is born inherently good and that humans become bad or destructive when the path to their full potential is blocked or frustrated. If this idea resonates with you, then it is easier to have compassion or empathy for your perceived antagonist. If revenge appears in your thoughts, recognize that these kinds of thoughts consume a significant portion of your energy, which could be used more constructively.

Identify and give up your personal antagonist. This is a competition that you cannot win. Just say no! Being your best True Self is more than good enough!

Mirrors & Fears

I want to be accepted for the person that I am and not be judged as something that I am not. How can I contribute to revealing my actual reality as a human being? Must I prove my acceptability as a thoughtful and caring human being? How do I deal (in a harmonious fashion) with those who are hidebound with false conclusions of me? How can I establish dialogue (to clarify and identify misgivings) with those who avoid having an open conversation? What is the spark that ignites the process of reconciliation? Do I give up on my beliefs and fight fire with fire -- a choice that is conflicted with my nature?

This is my issue to reconcile. There are those who have been led to believe that I am a person to fear and not worthy of meaningful connection. The carriers of these falsehoods continue to respond as if the falsehoods are true. On the surface, they seem assured of the validity of their misconceptions. I believe that in some cases, simmering below their level of awareness, they somehow sense that their conclusions are questionable. The net effect is that I have been ostracized from consideration and participation in a community -- where the actions of the community conflict with their expressed beliefs. Well-intended people circulate this negativity, explicitly or implicitly, to others but are not willing to express their feelings directly and honestly to the object of their discontent or wrath. I wonder what the true basis of their fear is. I wonder if they realize that their conclusions have an energy that is palpable to others and difficult to hide.

Trying to understand and resolve my issue, I start with what I believe to be true. When I was a young man taking a class, one of the principles taught was "we dislike in others what we dislike in ourselves." At that time, I thought that statement might be correct. There was a nice looking 60-year-old man who was always well dressed in my class. He was known to be a millionaire; however, it appeared that his nice clothing had hung in his closet for twenty years. For the first few weeks of that class, in my mind I would say, "You're a wealthy man; why not buy some better clothes?" Then one day the conversation in my mind changed; the question became, "Why don't I buy better clothes?" Of course, I had my excuses. At that time, I realized I was not so much concerned about my classmate's clothing; I didn't like what *I* was wearing. From those kinds of experiences, I learned that when I am unhappy with someone else and I can't identify the issue, I know that something below my level of awareness is itching for attention. In other words, we are our mirrors for each other.

My path to enlightenment has led me to another dilemma. What bothersome things am I reflecting to others (that they need to become aware of) that could enhance their own lives? Is it the fear of mistreatment they have experienced or observed? There are those who have habitual expectations of things going painfully wrong. They encourage others to make correct decisions and do the right thing to avoid pain. They may constantly encourage themselves to push down on the anger burning within. They try to protect others and become upset when others don't see things realistically - possibly a distraction from their own issues. This tendency can be the result of their own painful experiences and expectations that are internally driven and below their conscious awareness.

I am a mirror for others just as others have helped me see myself more clearly. I need to remember that our interaction with each other is part of our instinctual wholeness. Oneness is our reality - we are interconnected. My energy can express itself in subtle ways, such as sympathy for those who have blind spots in their perspectives. My contribution to creating a more harmonious relationship requires me to be on guard for any blind spots that I might have and to be open to what my mirror shows me for evaluation.

I am a very calm and peaceful person; therefore, I would not enjoy having a combative or accusatory conversation with anyone. For this reason, I tend to dance around when expressing my feelings, using analogies to make my point, simply because I do not want to create friction between myself and others. This approach to creating harmony with others is flawed. When my conversation does not directly express my feelings, the possibility of misinterpretation is enhanced. Therefore, I need to step out of my comfort zone by speaking directly to the issue with a harmonious perspective.

I know who I am, and I do not need adulation for me to feel good about myself. When I look at the conflict that is prominent in our world, I feel compelled to contribute as much as I can for the betterment of our planet. I realize peace begins with me as it does for anyone else.

I realize that there are those who are diseased or in poor health, who will not eat nutritiously to enhance the probability of recovery. When it is a loved one, it is difficult to deal with. And so it is with those who are locked into a perspective of the issue at hand. Everyone has the right to live their life in a way that they want to. Therefore, we can only support others in a way that they want to be supported. The lesson for me is that I can only do the best I can while searching for new solutions. My integrity, my passions require me to continue to engage in new ways of creating peace and harmony in the world around me. My goals for myself are:

- Always remember that harmony begins with me.
- Continue to express myself clearly and honestly.
- Continue to locate any blind spots in my life that I may have.
- Express sympathy for others, regardless if I lack understanding of what is driving their behavior.
- Listen carefully to understand the perspective of others.

> **We meet ourselves time and again in a thousand disguises on the paths of life.**
> – Carl Jung

The Masking of the Truth

Some of us have a positive outlook in life, while others have a tendency to look at life through a lens of what can go wrong. I consider myself a positive thinker, no matter how difficult the situation. I try to look for good in every situation. When dealing with tragedy, this can be a very challenging thing to do. For instance, the unexpected loss of a child is something that most parents never completely get over. Many grieving parents will try to support other children as a way of not allowing their child's death to be without purpose. It is their way of surviving the overwhelming pain of their loss.

I am one of those who tries to deal with negative situations knowing that there can be good in every situation. I am also aware that consciously, or unconsciously, ignoring reality can be harmful to oneself and invites harmful consequences. As a high school teacher, I was constantly thinking about how I could improve the lives of my students over and beyond my course requirements. My thinking engaged in the world of possibilities. At that time, there were many foreign students in our classrooms, speaking languages that we did not understand. I was told to find somebody in the classroom who spoke the same language. These were languages that I could not identify. Also, during that period of time, I had seven new students creating havoc throughout the school while failing all subjects. The school counselors did not know what to do with the students, and as a consequence, we were told to send the students directly to the principal's office.

One day, I invited the assistant principal to enter the back of my classroom and observe what was going on. For reasons unknown to me, he didn't show up. In the next class, I am sitting at my desk thinking about how I would like to work with my students to enhance their lives. I glanced down at the top of my left hand and noticed clear fluid rising up through my skin. I said to myself that this must be a manifestation of stress. I went to see my doctor that afternoon; my blood pressure was 160/100. My doctor asked me what the stress was related to. I stated that it was my work. My doctor told me that this job could kill me and not to go back to it. Although my health was excellent, my focus on the future of positive outcomes concealed the seriousness of my stress. I was oblivious to the amount of stress that I was suffering. As a consequence, I went to see the superintendent and informed him that this job was not compatible with my life. He changed my teaching position to one that allowed me to thrive and contribute to the well-being of students who were struggling.

If you were programmed as a child not to feel or acknowledge anger, it is possible you suppressed your anger by giving those feelings a different name, such as fear, upset or frustration. Yes, there are those who do not realize that they are actually very angry. Anger is a legitimate emotion. However, when we mislabel our feelings, it is difficult to resolve the related issue.

Feelings become locked into our bodies. These feelings are palpable and create problems. If one cannot account for feelings that are negatively impacting our life, it may be almost impossible to disarm them. The body/mind, working toward being all it can be, is trying to bring problem issues into the light of day and wants not to be ignored. The scientific information regarding Pavlov's dog and classical conditioning, or conditioning by association, demonstrates how easily humans can be conditioned in ways that are not always healthy.

It is not uncommon for females, who grew up with alcoholic and abusive fathers, to marry husbands with the same behavior patterns as their father. This is not motivated by wanting to be abused; it reflects the comfort zone that they experienced, even though it deeply wounded them. They will continue to form similar relationships until they understand the dynamics of their feelings. To combat the self-defeating feelings that are below their conscious awareness, an understanding of their family dynamics is necessary.

In common with doctors and auto mechanics is the idea that they must first diagnose the problem before they can fix it. And so it is with human behavior. Ernest Holmes is noted for saying, "treat (pray) but move your feet." Socrates tells us that a life unexamined is a life not worth living. There is a necessity to understand what is driving one's feelings and emotions in order to healthfully thrive.

Help! It's My Issue

Personal issues come in all shapes and sizes. The uniqueness of a personal issue reflects one's self in thoughts and actions. Your personal issues may be, or not be, bothersome and troublesome only for you. It may not be a problem for others, unless you try to make it so. When we make someone 'wrong', we have a recipe for an antagonistic relationship. This creates a situation where understanding, connection, and resolution remain elusive.

I have learned that when I have troublesome issues regarding someone else, to *any* degree, I will also discover that issue within myself. This is known as 'the mirror effect." Sometimes I am bothered about something in another person that I can't identify immediately. This uncomfortable feeling becomes the subject of a repeated conversation in my head. This conversation has energy around it. This energy attracts similar energy like a magnet. Sooner or later, this attracted energy will manifest in a way I can recognize. Once I identify the issue, I can recognize this issue as part of my own behavior that is uncomfortable within me, subconsciously.

Often, someone will magnify an issue, enabling one to see a lessor amount within one's self. I believe that one reason I am bothered by another is that this issue is also in me, below my level of awareness – and it doesn't feel comfortable as it seeks attention. It is analogous to an infection trying to work its way out of the body. For example, if I am bothered about how a specific person continually dominates conversations, I will become aware that I have perhaps done the same thing. This is a small indicator within me brought into conscious awareness by larger, outside demonstrations.

For me to resolve my issue with another person, I need to address the following considerations:

- Is my issue with another person any of my business?
- How does my issue with another person reflect in me?
- What good can be found in my personal issue?
- Would it be fruitful to recruit another person to defuse my issue?
- Or is it better to self-examine my issue and come up with alternatives that I can develop internally?
- Can I invite my antagonist to help me with my issue - without creating the perception of their being 'wrong'?
- How can I deal with my issue that is for the best and highest good for all concerned?

Dealing with personal issues that relate to others can be complex. Therefore, personal and thoughtful deliberations are imperative. One needs to consciously consider the possibilities of unintended consequences. If you are willing to accept responsibility for your connection to the issue, and take appropriate responsibility for its resolution, your efforts will be rewarded!

Baby Steps to Forgiveness

When forgiveness issues are not dealt with, we become easily distracted from focusing on one's True Self. This gives power to someone else over the direction of one's life, and therefore, we will blame them for the consequences. We become blinded to the personal issues that negatively impact our life, and thus our ability to live as our true selves remains in jeopardy.

There are people who want to forgive and can't. Others lack the desire to forgive the object of their grievance. Within that deep and long-held grievance is overwhelming emotional pain that has significantly impacted one's life. In effect, this grievance becomes one's personal antagonist. This negative energy creates an obstacle for one to focus on. The pain of a deeply held grievance can be extremely difficult to overcome; therefore, forgiveness may be the only solution. It is easy to turn the lights on; just flip the switch. But one cannot flip a magic, emotional switch and all is forgiven. However, there is a process one can consider to forgiving oneself and others. It takes time to learn and absorb the following steps, but the benefits are many.

The baby steps towards forgiveness include an understanding of the development of human interaction. If you can see that the general developmental pattern of human behavior applies to you as well as to others, then the door to forgiveness opens a little wider.

As a practical matter, hanging onto your grievance may be more harmful to you then the object of your grievance. The person related to your grievance may not even be aware of your stress in this regard.

Humanistic psychologist, Abraham Maslow, believed that everyone is born inherently good. However, when the path to their full potential was frustrated or blocked, they became angry, fearful and/ or destructive.

It is well known that we cannot walk in someone else's shoes. If one is dealing with someone who is demonstrating harmful behavior, sympathy or empathy may be required. This is not to say that one should accept physical abuse. In general, most of our human behavior patterns were formed in childhood. Often these patterns and unique perspectives remain operative in adulthood.

In addition, acceptable behavior patterns in children may not be acceptable as a course of action in adults. As an example: If one was told how much they were loved while somebody was beating on them, one would tend to have a strong, adverse reaction to the word "love." Without knowing this person's background information, this extreme reaction would make little sense to others. Sometimes compassion is required when dealing with others that we do not know well. Making assumptions about others is a risky business. The chances of making a correct assumption may be significantly less than 50 percent.

Most of us have regrets about our own past behavior. We relive past events and repeatedly contemplate what we could have done better. There are those who are less forgiving of themselves than of their family, friends and acquaintances. I believe that everyone strives to do the best that they can at their level of awareness. As humans, we generally strive to do better. With lessons learned, our level of awareness increases our understanding of self and others. When we hang on to our past indiscretions and do not acknowledge our limited awareness at that time, we tend not to be forgiving of ourselves. Ultimately, this can be a heavy, unnecessary burden for us to carry.

If you can't forgive yourself, it is very difficult (if not impossible) to forgive others!

The act of forgiveness does not necessarily include condoning the actions of others. It is simply an acknowledgement that each of us should reach for an awareness of our own reality.

Baby Steps to Forgiveness:

1. Recognize the impact of difficult situations on children raised in situations that are not conducive to becoming a well-adjusted adult.

2. Everyone is trying to do the best they can at their current level of awareness. Everyone is not on identical levels of awareness.

3. Learn to forgive yourself. From birth to death, we are in a learning environment called the School of Life.

4. When situations are not completely understood, have empathy or sympathy for others, as well as yourself.

5. Accepting the concept of Oneness supports the idea that everyone is interconnected. Therefore, any thought or activity that separates us from others is conflicted with our natural way to be.

The Blessing in Suffering

There is value in human suffering. When one begins to sense the suffering in life and, at the same time, begins to awaken to deeper realties, a shift occurs - one's complacency regarding our normal illusions about reality can be re-evaluated. Our sense of what is real and what is important starts to change. I do not know anyone who enjoys suffering, including me! However, there are those who *appear* to enjoy it. Apparently, they are trying to fulfill an unconscious need indirectly. Suffering is part of our human experience. It can be a pathway to a deeper understanding of one's True Self and our human potential.

My experience of polio was my big blessing. I was in the seventh grade when I was hospitalized. I was paralyzed from the waist down and not able to lift my legs. My doctors told me that they would help me as best they could; however, I would be crippled. This was a very painful physical experience and continued for many years in the form of leg cramps. I was fortunate that because of my young age, I didn't think about what the doctors had said; I was focused on getting out of the hospital and being able to do the things I wanted to do. I lived in my head and kept busy with things I enjoyed while going through intensive therapy.

At that time, I lacked a reasonable amount of self-confidence. However, there was a big blessing connected with this medical experience. Below my conscious level of awareness, I learned that regardless of what someone tells me, I can achieve my goals. This became clear as I now look back on my life. As one of many examples: Some of the well-intentioned adults in my life informed me that I was not suitably equipped to be a student at the University of Illinois. This assessment may have seemed correct at the time; however, I currently have two degrees from that institution. Suffering can provide a deeper and more satisfying sense of self. It asks you to dig a little deeper into your True Self. The ultimate question relates to who you really are. The answer to this requires more than an intellectual activity. Although a complete understanding may lie below one's conscious awareness, there remains a drive within, towards satisfying one's passions, that seeks to emerge.

When all is well we tend not to be introspective. Why would one examine their life if they are basically content with their current situation? On the conscious surface, many things can appear to be satisfactory. Below one's conscious awareness, there is a drive to connect with one's True Self. Too often it takes a tragedy before we search more deeply for answers. *Who am I?* and *What is my purpose?*

are two questions that can surface. The answers to these kinds of questions can only come when we focus within.

Our suffering can smash to pieces the complacency of our normal illusions about reality, force us to become alive in a special sense, to see carefully, to feel deeply, to get in touch with ourselves in ways we have avoided. Some say that suffering is the first grace. In a special sense, suffering is almost a time of rejoicing, for it marks the birth of creative insight. It allows us to know ourselves at our core.

When suffering is experienced, some of us do not automatically search within for a solution. For me, I was never the same after dealing with suffering or experiencing a tragedy. I wondered *What is wrong with me?* while trying to understand what I was experiencing. However, there are those who have similar experiences who retained and deepened their previous beliefs about the world around them; they "dug in their heels." This unwillingness to look within themselves maintained their chronic condition. In a sense, they remain asleep to the possibilities of a satisfying life. For some, the fear of change, the fear of loss or the fear of finding out something negative about themselves is a contributing factor.

I do not advocate setting yourself up to suffer. Nor do I believe that anyone should be complacent when suffering. However, suffering is part of life. Suffering can be used as a wake-up call to shift one's attention to more significant and deeper realities. Consider it an alarm bell to focus one's attention on more significant uses of time, thoughts and actions. If we are oblivious to our true nature, we cannot fully live life. Focusing primarily on material wealth, power or status may never fully satisfy you. True happiness and fulfillment is only possible when living in alignment with your True Self.

Understanding Healing
through Oneness

Healing is created by balancing the body's energies so that it can function normally. It makes little difference *how* the body's energies are properly balanced. A doctor's role is to set the parameters for the body to heal itself. Doctors do not heal; it is the body itself which performs the healing process. There is nothing beyond the power of the body's own healing process. There are countless kinds of modalities that can help create a healing. With a cut on our hands, provided we clean it and protect it, the body heals it. Therefore, one can conclude that the body is designed to heal itself. However, when the body experiences extreme stresses, other measures may be needed to overcome the imbalance.

The concept of Oneness acknowledges that we do not live in a linear universe. Everything is reacting to everything else instantaneously.

Once we recognize that reality, other healing modalities become more relatable. There is more than one way to get to Chicago and it makes no difference where you start from. There is more than one way to create a healing. It can be a physical approach, such as surgery or physical conditioning. Or it can be a mental approach, such as using a therapist, meditation, or learning to understand your true nature and who you are, etc. Thoughts are a source of energy which can be used to enhance a healing. When we recognize the nature of Oneness, it makes sense that a path to healing can be created in different ways. Each cell, organ or system has an action or function, vibration, odor, etc. If one of these characteristics is brought back into normalcy, the other characteristics tend to follow.

What we believe is an important aspect of selecting the best path to follow. The body follows the mind. The words and thoughts used regarding one's self and others are important. If one refers to oneself as having a bad limb, organ etc., it succumbs to the idea that that their body may not return to normalcy. Words have energies with intentions that are invoked. There is a school of thought that promotes the idea that the subconscious mind does not deal with jokes and processes them more literally: "This is just killing me..." Words can be used as tools to give direction to where one is going. For example: If I am feeling poorly and someone asked me, "How are you?" my reply would indicate not so much my present condition but where I am going: "Alert, alive, enthusiastic and feeling good!" Words are tools!

Unmet expectations, whether self-generated or set by others, can be a major distraction to one's good health. This creates an obstacle to dealing with one's True Self. Living as one's True Self enhances a healthier lifestyle. It also enhances the probability of living in harmony with your environment. Why? You are unique, with a role to play that is bigger than yourself, which supports your well-being as well as contributing to a cause greater than yourself – Oneness.

Man is a structural, chemical, spiritual and psychological being. There must be a balance between the four, otherwise imbalances will be the consequence, limiting one's ability to thrive. Although we are mainly water, we are physically constructed with the same elements found on the planet.

Without a holistic approach to healing, the underlying cause of an illness is not considered. If one understands the underlying cause of their illness, it can offer hope and a new way of dealing with their health. Listening to the stories of those who are suffering has healing ingredients/properties. Knowing that someone cares about you is important. The sense that you are not alone on your journey is a natural/organic medicine.

The Case Against Fighting Cancer

Understanding the nature of Oneness helps to reveal that good can be found in everything and everywhere. And so, it is with illness. Blessings are where you find them. Pain is an alarm bell indicating something is out of balance. The associated illness/cancer has a message for you. Your structure, energetic chemistry and your spiritual/psychological stance are out of balance and need appropriate attention. It is difficult to solve a problem if the driving impetus is not understood. We have internal guidance that can help direct us to the needed information. But first, we must learn how to use and trust it. Embracing cancer as an added benefit to your life adds to the possibility of enhancing your life spiritually as well as physically. In other words, getting to the underlying source/cause of cancer enhances one's ability to heal. Focusing on your lesson to be learned, and knowing that you are whole, complete and heading toward manifestation as such, is part of the healing process.

There are various modalities/techniques that can provide the information you need. Kinesiology techniques communicate directly with the body and may have the answers to your questions. Some other examples and techniques are medical professionals, mental health professionals, meditation, prayer, books and holistic healers using various modalities. I consider myself my primary doctor who uses the expertise of others. In other words, if you can't swim, take a boat. Just make sure you push off from shore toward your healing.

CREATING YOUR PATH

Transitioning the In-Between Times

I believe that I am an intelligent and deserving person. I try to be a good and a helpful person. Why is it that my desires and dreams do not manifest themselves? Am I not good enough or smart enough? What is wrong with me? What do I need to understand?

In-Between Times

Sometimes we find ourselves living in the In-Between Times. When we are no longer who we used to be, and not yet at our next stage of development. Anything that is alive grows and, therefore, changes. A transition period can be unsettling because of the unfamiliar or unknown future - being in an unfamiliar space can create fear. Fear of not being secure. Transition refers to a state of change. My thoughts and actions as a child are no longer appropriate as an adult. These kinds of observations may be, or not, obvious to oneself. According to Socrates it is important to examine one's own life. If you carefully examine your life, the possibility of finding inconsistencies in your beliefs and your actions become important to living a successful and fulfilled life.

Sometimes there needs to be time and opportunity for peripheral things to coalesce prior to activating your dreams. Many of these peripheral activities you may not be aware of. *Have you ever received help that was not expected from a source that was not expected?* The supporting energies that you may need require certain conditions for the manifestation of your desires. You may not be aware of everything you need to fulfill your dream. The energy of your thoughts will attract appropriate energies from sources that you may not be aware of in order to support you. In addition, you may need time to reassess what is important to you, what will provide your best outcome.

Creativity and choice are two of the greatest gifts that humans have to manifest a satisfying life. Creative ideas do not always come instantaneously. It appears that time does not necessarily correlate with great ideas. Whatever amount of time it takes to generate a helpful idea is exactly what is required. Sometimes choices need to be made between more than one good idea. Therefore, in the In-Between Times, it can be considered a blessing for your thoughts and ideas to have an adequate amount of time to coalesce into the best outcome for you. What appears to be a disappointment may be bringing you a blessing.

Physicists tell us that everything is a form of energy. Thoughts are a form of energy. Thoughts are not visible by the naked eye. If you switch from happy thoughts to sad thoughts, you can feel the shift in your body. An analogy can be made between the actions generated by one's thoughts and the energetic action in a seed. When a seed is planted, it grows at a pace compatible with its environment. There are variables such as water, nutrients, temperature and space to grow that affect the quality and quantity of the seed's potential. And so, it is for the seedling for your dreams.

Work your way through the In-Between Times through these actions:

- Count your blessings! You may be surprised with how many you have, and you can express gratitude for them. This is an attracting energy that can bring more of the same into your life.
- Be aware of the times when you may feel that unexplainable things occur that support your endeavors.
- Keep the faith! The universe conspires for everything to reach its full potential.

Energy works in mysterious ways!
Many things can offer you a challenge
to becoming your True Self.

The Journey is the Destination

Our journey is the destination because it is interactive with the creative evolutionary energy of the universe. Life itself is a process of change. Anything that is alive is growing, and therefore, is changing. This energy conspires for everything to reach its full potential. Quantum physics tells us that every set of circumstances is driven by its potential. Therefore, learning to live in harmony with this change is exceedingly important. When we resist this energy or lack an understanding of it, unintended and undesirable consequences become more probable. Modern physics describes the universe as interactive energies from birth to maturity.

Well-intended individuals steadfastly hang on to false assumptions that are not fully true. There are those who express that humans have little to do with climate change. They remained hidebound to what they believe. Each of us must challenge our own personal beliefs.

Our beliefs have a significant role to play in our personal conflicts. No doubt this is a challenging task that requires much effort and dedication. Some would say it is part of the human condition. Plants and trees are always reaching upward for the sunlight to be all they can be - a never-ending process.

Who am I? is a question that each of us must consider. Possibly this is the most important and significant question to be resolved. If our assumptions about oneself and others is incorrect, creating a peaceful and prosperous community may not be possible. I believe that most of the troubling issues in society can be attributed to individuals not knowing who they really are - their True Self. One of the characteristics of this condition is fear. Fear creates uncertainty and anxiety, while looking outside oneself for a scapegoat. This is the foundational issue that must be resolved before harmony can be a signature of our community.

Getting to one's True Self can seem like a lifelong process; however, it can be expedited with intention and effort. There are many ways to connect with one's True Self. It is up to you to research and explore the possibilities and processes that resonate with you. This is something that only you can do for yourself. You would be contributing to something greater than yourself as an added benefit.

Be knowledgeable about current significant issues. Do not assume that you can walk in someone else's shoes and fully understand their perspective. Learn what the perspective is on each end of the continuum. If you rely solely on one or two sources of information, it is unlikely that you will have a complete perspective on the reality of the subject. Humans who have similar beliefs tend to cluster together and disregard other perspectives. This tendency is a distraction from finding common ground with other belief systems; therefore, separation from other perspectives is inevitable and creates a 'them vs. us' scenario.

Effective conversation is not characterized by bullying or dominating conversations. That is a recipe for separation of perspectives with little possibility of finding common ground. Enlightening conversations are enhanced when both parties are listening to learn the perspective of the other, without including a personal agenda. Selective listening will not allow a better understanding of what is being expressed.

Our political dynamics reflect how dysfunctional our government becomes when selective listening becomes the norm. Our government leaders and their views reflect the general population. The words we use are important. Fighting is a common expression for what one supports. Fighting includes offense and defense, where one side must dominate the other - a situation where finding common ground is less likely. Let's take fighting out of our political and personal agendas.

All problems have a core element of fear that is often below one's level of awareness. Under this condition, understanding the driving dynamics of an issue is not probable and is misleading. As a counseling technique for oneself or others, simply ask what fear is connected to the issue. Getting to the core of an issue can allow effective and unifying ideas to surface. It allows us to expand our personal identity into a more unified identity, i.e. the concept of Oneness.

Expecting perfection may not be possible in a dynamic world that is constantly changing. Although it may be good to strive for perfection, it is not an end goal because we live in a world that is continuously driven by a creative evolutionary energy. Our goal should be to live in harmony with All There Is.

> ***The planet is alive, nothing is stationary***
> ***and change is inevitable!***

The Path to an Extraordinary Life

From birth to maturity, life can be looked at as a series of experiences. These experiences influence how we view and respond to life. If you were isolated on a small island with coconut trees and a monkey, your experiences would be significantly limited. What could you know or understand about the dynamics of the world? With an increase of new and varied experiences, our creative nature is also expanded. Our passion and curiosity to reach our full potential is immensely expanded. Our list of choices becomes much longer.

Humans try to avoid experiencing illness or personal tragedy. It doesn't feel good, and we do not consciously pursue these experiences. The question then: *Is there some positive value to be gained in tragedy?* I say yes; there is good that can be found in everything. There are parents who tragically lost a child and found their ability to cope by helping other children. There are recovering drug/alcohol addicts who enhance their recovery by helping others do the same. Sadness and tragedy are part of our human experience. Difficult experiences can take us deeper into ourselves, with a deeper appreciation of how precious and fleeting life can be. It can dramatically affect one's perspective and re-prioritize what is most important.

The universe conspires with everything to reach its full potential. A blade of grass works its way up in the cracks of cement. Its goal is to be all it can be - driven by its potential.

The path to an extraordinary life includes all our experiences. Experiences that are deemed undesirable do not preclude one's journey to their full potential. There are blessings to be found in suffering that offer understanding and emotional awakening that are difficult to access any other way.

There are many of us who have learned to use and trust our internal guidance/ intuition. However, there are those who question why, at times, their life doesn't appear to be working very well, based upon perceived negative experiences. If you are following your internal guidance, why would it take you to a place that you don't want to be? If you consider that any decision that one makes can result in countless unintended consequences, you begin to realize the limitations to leftbrain thinking only. Our mind is not capable of sorting out all possibilities; it is too complex. Consider the idea that it is possible for a negative experience to lead to a positive outcome further down the road - something that is more significant and valued in your life.

Our journey into an extraordinary life can be greatly enhanced by a fuller range of experiences. Trust in our guidance that we are in the right place and at the right time, which contributes to our highest good. Yes, it is faith in one's belief system, and the knowledge that one's thoughts are creating directed energies that support your endeavors. It can be understood as a collaboration of energies that supports your extraordinary life. Our internal guidance can take you beyond your fondest dreams - possibly to a big, wonderful surprise! Life is a journey that you can enjoy.

Experiencing difficulties can enhance your extraordinary life!

Daily Practices That Can Enhance an Extraordinary Life

What do you want to become? Who do you want to be? These are questions that only you can answer. Whatever your response is, it is up to you to engage in a practice that brings you competence in the area that you choose. With adequate repetition and proper techniques, you will develop mental and muscle memory - sometimes known as internalization. Once something has been internalized, it becomes part of one's way of being, naturally.

Modern physics tells us that everything is energy, everything is connected by energy; therefore, everything is one. There is no separation of anything in the universe. It also tells us that we do not live in a linear universe; everything is interacting with everything instantaneously. Another principle is that energy cannot be created or destroyed, only transformed. *Entanglement,* a term used in physics, describes that things previously connected maintain an energetic connection regardless of space or time. This demonstrates that separation is not totally possible. Therefore, the concept of Oneness becomes relatable.

Migrating birds do not use maps to get to their destination. They have an internal guidance system that is directly connected to the planet's energy systems. And so, it is with humans.

Recommended Daily Practices

1. Maintain the Oneness concept in everything you think and do.
2. Activity engage your internal guidance/intuition in all areas of your life.
3. Continually search for your core identity. Know who you are and the passions of your soul.
4. Always embody integrity; be a product of your word.
5. Follow your deepest passions.
6. Remember to express gratitude. The energy of love overcomes resistance.

CLOSING THOUGHTS

Learning is a necessary lifelong process that allows us to thrive and prosper in a changing environment. Life itself is continuously growing and, therefore, changing. There is something within you that seeks answers to your questions. This drive for information is a process of directing you towards what you need to know to enhance your life. Your life represents part of the evolutionary drive of consciousness in the universe. Yes, you are part of it. Creativity is a big part of human nature; it is what we do.

We do not always know the effect we have on others. As a school teacher, I was often amazed when years later, students stopped by to visit. They would tell me their stories and what they learned in my classes that was beneficial to their lives. The interesting thing was that what they learned was sometimes only incidentally connected to what I was teaching. Your good intentions, when interacting with others, can spark unintentional goodwill. Therefore, what you do is important to enhancing a world that works for everyone.

You can only be your best self. There's no other one just like you. Therefore, your competition in life is between you and your best self. This is key to personal fulfillment.

Each of us has a unique DNA and varied life experiences. Therefore, if you believe exactly everything that I believe, I would worry about you. Remember the Socrates mandate: *A life unexamined is a life not worth living.*

Following your internal guidance will sometimes offer you difficult things to experience. It is important to remember that your internal guidance evaluates your left-brain activities, your right-brain activities, conscious mind, subconscious mind and the passion of your soul in its calculation for your path to follow. Just because you experience difficulties does not necessarily mean that you are off a guided path to your full potential. You can learn from difficult experiences that will enhance your life.

Not knowing where you will exactly end up in life can be intimidating. Life can be considered a mystery to engage. Life can become more exciting when you realize that your path can take you beyond your most treasured dreams into your full potential that is fulfilling and peaceful.

Picture life as a journey through the beautiful landscape of the planet. Can you see yourself on this journey through the forest, along the rivers, and hills? Sometimes the sun is shining, sometimes it is pouring rain. Occasionally there is an obstacle in our path that is difficult to cross, but we make it. Sometimes we feel lost, not sure which direction to travel. What will happen next? Our internal guidance gives us a path to follow and then we become safe. Think of what it will be like when we get to the top of the mountain, gazing at the landscape below. Noticing areas of rain and areas of sunshine with cleaning rays of light penetrating the landscape and rainbows extending from the mountains. We see the great beauty of our journey and understand it was well worth it. A sense of peace and contentment floods our inner self.

Your life is your gift to share. Enjoy it!

AUTHOR'S BIOGRAPHY

Charles Albert "Al" Huth was born and raised in Chicago. He received a Bachelor of Science in Education and a Master in Education from the University of Illinois, Champaign/Urbana. He also worked on a Ph.D. in research, testing and measurement while teaching junior high and high school, a profession he enjoyed for many years. Later, as his interests shifted, he trained as a massage therapist, Touch for

Health practitioner and kinesiologist, building a practice in southern California. Holistic healing remains a major focus of his professional life, though he definitely considers himself primarily a teacher. After moving to southern Oregon, he has immersed himself in teaching classes at OLLI at Southern Oregon University, and writing articles and books on healing, metaphysical, and motivational subjects.

The author has facilitated classes regarding living an extraordinary life, with processes and concepts. These were interactive classes that influenced the approach and perspective of the teacher. He has anecdotal stories that add confirmation to the value of his work. He has already published three books on this topic: *Living an Extraordinary Life - The Magic of Oneness; Essentials for a Changing World - Living Harmoniously with Yourself and Others;* and *The Evolving Higher Self: A Directed Guide to Fulfillment.*

He has a wide range of interests and a passion for helping others. Networking and co-creating new concepts and processes that have personal and global implications for peace is a calling close to his heart. He is also a professionally trained magician.

The author is available for speaking engagements and workshops based upon any of his books. Please contact Mr. Huth through his website: www.infinitemagician@sbcglobal.net

Printed in the United States
By Bookmasters